MARRIAGE

Love and Life in the Divine Plan

A Pastoral Letter of the
United States Conference of Catholic Bishops

United States Conference of Catholic Bishops
Washington, D.C.

Marriage: Life and Love in the Divine Plan was developed by the Committee on Laity, Marriage, Family Life, and Youth of the United States Conference of Catholic Bishops (USCCB). It was approved by the full body of the USCCB at its November 2009 General Meeting and has been authorized for publication by the undersigned.

Msgr. David J. Malloy, STD
General Secretary, USCCB

First Printing, December 2009

ISBN 978-1-60137-092-1

CONTENTS

———————————— ◯◯ ————————————

About the Cover

This image of the Wedding Feast at Cana, written by contemporary artist and iconographer Vladimir Grygorenko, depicts the major elements of the familiar story from the Gospel of John (2:1-11). At right, the head waiter tells the groom, seated beside the bride, that the good wine has been kept until last. The second man on the right represents the wedding guests, who do not understand the meaning of what has transpired. In the foreground, the server pours the water at Christ's command, and at left, Mary converses with Christ. This conversation shows forth Christ's desire to help the married couple at Mary's request, and it is central to the meaning of the piece.

INTRODUCTION: THE BLESSING AND GIFT OF MARRIAGE

———————— ⚭ ————————

Blessed be the God and Father of our Lord Jesus Christ,
who has blessed us in Christ with every spiritual blessing in
the heavens. (Eph 1:3)

Among the many blessings that God has showered upon us in Christ is the blessing of marriage, a gift bestowed by the Creator from the creation of the human race. His hand has inscribed the vocation to marriage in the very nature of man and woman (see Gn 1:27-28, 2:21-24).

Father, by your plan man and woman are united,
and married life has been established
as the one blessing that was not forfeited by original sin
or washed away by the flood.[1]

Original Sin introduced evil and disorder into the world. As a consequence of the break with God, this first sin ruptured the original communion between man and woman. Nonetheless, the original blessing of marriage was never revoked.

Jesus Christ has not only restored the original blessing in its fullness but elevated it by making marriage between baptized

---

1 Nuptial Blessing, *Rite of Marriage* A, no. 33, in *The Rites of the Catholic Church* (New York: Pueblo Publishing, 1976). All subsequent texts from the Rite of Marriage refer to this edition.

Christians a sacramental sign of his own love for the Church—as we hear proclaimed in the wedding liturgy:

> Father, to reveal the plan of your love,
> you made the union of husband and wife
> an image of the covenant between you and your people.
> In the fulfillment of this sacrament,
> the marriage of Christian man and woman
> is a sign of the marriage between Christ and the Church.[2]

While marriage is a special blessing for Christians because of the grace of Christ, marriage is also a natural blessing and gift for everyone in all times and cultures. It is a source of blessing to the couple, to their families, and to society and includes the wondrous gift of co-creating human life. Indeed, as Pope John Paul II never tired of reminding us, the future of humanity depends on marriage and the family.[3] It is just such a conviction that has led us, the Catholic bishops of the United States, to write this pastoral letter.

We rejoice that so many couples are living in fidelity to their marital commitment. We thank them for proclaiming in their daily lives the beauty, goodness, and truth of marriage. In countless ways, both ordinary and heroic, through good times and bad, they bear witness to the gift and blessing they have received from the hand of their Creator. We are grateful, too, for all those who work with young people and engaged couples to establish good marriages, who help married couples to grow in love and strengthen their union, and who help those in crisis to resolve their problems and bring healing to their lives.

At the same time we are troubled by the fact that far too many people do not understand what it means to say that marriage—both as a natural institution and a Christian

---

2   Nuptial Blessing, *Rite of Marriage B*, no. 120.

3   See Pope John Paul II, *On the Family* (*Familiaris Consortio* [FC]) (Washington, DC: United States Conference of Catholic Bishops [USCCB], 1982), no. 75: "The future of the world and of the church passes through the family." See also FC, no. 86.

sacrament—is a blessing and gift from God. We observe, for example, that some people esteem marriage as an ideal but can be reluctant to make the actual commitment necessary to enter and sustain it. Some choose instead to live in cohabiting relationships that may or may not lead to marriage and can be detrimental to the well-being of themselves and any children.

In addition, the incidence of divorce remains high. The social sanctions and legal barriers to ending one's marriage have all but disappeared, and the negative effects of divorce on children, families, and the community have become more apparent in recent decades.

We are alarmed that a couple's responsibility to serve life by being open to children is being denied and abandoned more frequently today. Couples too often reflect a lack of understanding of the purposes of marriage. There is a loss of belief in the value of those purposes when couples readily treat, as separate choices, the decisions to get married and to have children. This indicates a mentality in which children are seen not as integral to a marriage but as optional. When children are viewed in this way, there can be damaging consequences not only for them but also for the marriage itself.

We note a disturbing trend today to view marriage as a mostly private matter, an individualistic project not related to the common good but oriented mostly to achieving personal satisfaction.

Finally, we bishops feel compelled to speak out against all attempts to redefine marriage so that it would no longer be exclusively the union of a man and a woman as God established and blessed it in the natural created order.

The opportunities and urgencies of the present moment are many and varied. Nearly thirty years ago, Pope John Paul II summoned the Church to meet a challenge that has become even more important today:

> At a moment of history in which the family is the object of numerous forces that seek to destroy it or in some way to deform it, and aware that the well-being of society and her

own good are intimately tied to the good of the family, the church perceives in a more urgent and compelling way her mission of proclaiming to all people the plan of God for marriage and the family, ensuring their full vitality and human and Christian development, and thus contributing to the renewal of society and of the people of God.[4]

The task of proclamation to which the Holy Father refers is one that we bishops exercise today as teachers and pastors, specifically in this pastoral letter. We address the pastoral letter first and foremost to the Catholic faithful in the United States. We call upon them to stand against all attacks on marriage and to stand up for the meaning, dignity, and sanctity of marriage and the family. In a spirit of witness and service we also offer our message to all men and women in the hope of inspiring them to embrace this teaching.

We intend this pastoral letter to be a theological and doctrinal foundation. It can be a resource to help and encourage all those who are moving toward marriage, who are journeying in married life, and who are accompanying and assisting those who are called to the vocation of marriage.

Our pastoral letter presents those beliefs and teachings of the Catholic Church—informed by human reason and enlightened by Divine Revelation—that summarize and express God's plan for marriage. This divine plan, like the gift of marriage itself, is something we receive, not something we construct or change to fit our purposes. It is a firm foundation, a truthful guide, a trustworthy light for the way.

For all who seek to find *meaning in* their marriage will do so when they are open to accepting the transcendent *meaning of* marriage according to God's plan. Of this quest for meaning and truth, Pope Benedict XVI writes:

All people feel the interior impulse to love authentically: love and truth never abandon them completely, because these are

---

4   FC, no. 3.

4

the vocation planted by God in the heart and mind of every human person. The search for love and truth is purified and liberated by Jesus Christ from the impoverishment that our humanity brings to it, and he reveals to us in all its fullness the initiative of love and the plan for true life that God has prepared for us.[5]

Our pastoral letter is an invitation to discover, or perhaps rediscover, the blessing given when God first established marriage as a natural institution and when Christ restored and elevated it as a sacramental sign of salvation.

---

5   Pope Benedict XVI, *Charity in Truth* (*Caritas in Veritate*) (Washington, DC: USCCB, 2009), no. 1.

PART ONE:
MARRIAGE IN THE
ORDER OF CREATION
The Natural Institution of Marriage

What Is Marriage?

Marriage is a lifelong partnership of the whole of life, of mutual and exclusive fidelity, established by mutual consent between a man and a woman, and ordered towards the good of the spouses and the procreation of offspring.[6] As the Second Vatican Council reminds us, marriage is not a purely human institution: "the intimate partnership of life and the love which constitutes the married state has been established by the creator and endowed by him with its own proper laws. . . . For God himself is the author of marriage."[7] Moreover, God has endowed marriage with certain essential attributes, without which marriage cannot exist as he intends.

The Church has taught through the ages that marriage is an exclusive relationship between one man and one woman. This

---

6   See *Catechism of the Catholic Church* (2nd ed.) (CCC) (Washington, DC: Libreria Editrice Vaticana–USCCB, 2000), no. 1601; *Code of Canon Law: Latin-English Edition: New English Translation* (*Codex Iuris Canonici* [CIC]) (Washington, DC: Canon Law Society of America, 1998), cc. 1055.1, 1056-1057; *Code of Canons of the Eastern Churches: New English Translation* (*Codex Canonum Ecclesiarum Orientalum* [CCEO]) (Washington, DC: Canon Law Society of America, 2001), c. 776 §§1, 3, and c. 817.

7   Second Vatican Council, *Constitution on the Church in the Modern World* (*Gaudium et Spes* [GS]), no. 48, in *Vatican Council II: The Basic Sixteen Documents*, ed. Austin Flannery (Northport, NY: Costello Publishing, 1996). All subsequent citations of Vatican II documents refer to this edition.

union, once validly entered and consummated, gives rise to a bond that cannot be dissolved by the will of the spouses.[8] Marriage thus created is a faithful, privileged sphere of intimacy between the spouses that lasts until death.

Marriage is not merely a private institution, however. It is the foundation for the family, where children learn the values and virtues that will make good Christians as well as good citizens. The importance of marriage for children and for the upbringing of the next generation highlights the importance of marriage for all society.

Conjugal love, the love proper to marriage, is present in the commitment to the complete and total gift of self between husband and wife. Conjugal love establishes a unique communion of persons through the relationship of mutual self-giving and receiving between husband and wife, a relationship by which "a man leaves his father and mother and clings to his wife, and the two of them become one body [flesh]" (Gn 2:24).

The Second Vatican Council speaks about conjugal love in words of great beauty:

> The Lord, wishing to bestow special gifts of grace and divine love on married love, has restored, perfected, and elevated it. A love like that, bringing together the human and the divine, leads the partners to a free and mutual self-giving, experienced in tenderness and action, and permeating their entire lives; this love is actually developed and increased by its generous exercise.[9]

As Part Two of this pastoral letter will examine, in conjugal love one can see something of how Christ loves his Church (Eph 5:25).

---

8   CIC, cc. 1056, 1134, 1141; CCEO, cc. 776 §3, 853.

9   GS, no. 49.

Male-Female Complementarity
Is Essential to Marriage

God created man in his image,
in the divine image he created him;
male and female he created them. (Gn 1:27)

The two creation stories in the book of Genesis communicate two important truths about the identity of man and woman and the relationship between them. In the first account, God creates both male and female at the same time and in the divine image. This act completes creation, and God judges it to be "very good" (Gn 1:31). In this way, Sacred Scripture affirms the fundamental equality and dignity of man and woman as persons created in God's image.

The second creation account emphasizes that both sexes are necessary for God's plan. Having created Adam, God says, "It is not good for the man to be alone" (Gn 2:18). So God creates a helpmate who is suitable for him and matches him. "Helpmate" (*ezer*) is a word reserved in the Bible not for inferiors but most often for God himself, who is Israel's "helper." Indeed, after God creates all of the animals and brings them to Adam to name, it becomes clear that none of them is "the suitable partner for the man" (Gn 2:20).

Then God puts Adam under a deep sleep and, using one of his ribs, builds up a woman for him as a suitable partner or helpmate. When he sees the woman, Adam cries out in wondrous joy:

> This one, at last, is bone of my bones
> > and flesh of my flesh;
> This one shall be called "woman" [*ishah*],
> > for out of "her man" [*ish*] this one has been
> > taken. (Gn 2:23)

Adam and Eve were literally made for each other. Man and woman have been made to come together in the union of marriage. The text of Genesis continues: "That is why a man leaves his father and mother and clings to his wife, and the two of them become one body [flesh]" (Gn 2:24).

Marriage, this clinging together of husband and wife as one flesh, is based on the fact that man and woman are both different and the same. They are different as male and female, but the same as human persons who are uniquely suited to be partners or help-mates for each other. The difference between man and woman, however, cannot be restricted to their bodies, as if the body could be separated from the rest of the human person. The human person is a union of body and soul as a single being. Man and woman are two different ways of being a human person.

While man and woman are different, their differences serve to relate them to each other. They are not different in a parallel way, as two lines that never meet. Man and woman do not have separate destinies. They are related to each other precisely in their differences.

The differences between male and female are complementary. Male and female are distinct bodily ways of being human, of being open to God and to one another—two distinct yet harmonizing ways of responding to the vocation to love.

While human persons are more than biological organisms, the roots of marriage can be seen in the biological fact that a man and a woman can come together as male and female in a union that has the potential for bringing forth another human person. This kind of union fills the need for the continuation of the human race. Since human beings exist at more than a biological level, however, this union has further personal and spiritual dimensions. Marriage does not exist solely for the reproduction of another member of the species, but for the creation of a communion of persons.

To form a communion of persons is the vocation of everyone. As Pope John Paul II teaches, all human persons are created in the image of God, who is a communion of love of three persons, and thus all are called to live in a communion of self-giving love: "to say that man is created in the image and likeness of God means that man is called to exist 'for' others, to become a gift."[10]

Marriage, however, is a unique communion of persons. In their intimate union as male and female, the spouses are called to exist for each other. Just as Genesis describes Eve as a helper for Adam, we can see that in marriage, a husband and wife are meant to help each other through self-giving. "In the 'unity of the two,' man and woman are called from the beginning not only to exist 'side by side' or 'together,' but they are also called *to exist mutually 'one for the other.'*"[11]

This communion of persons has the potential to bring forth human life and thus to produce the family, which is itself another kind of communion of persons and which is the origin and foundation of all human society. It is precisely the difference between man and woman that makes possible this unique communion of persons, the unique partnership of life and love that is marriage. A man and woman united in marriage as husband and wife serve as a symbol of both life and love in a way that no other relationship of human persons can.

The Two Ends or Purposes of Marriage

Marriage has two fundamental ends or purposes towards which it is oriented, namely, the good of the spouses as well as the procreation of children. Thus, the Church teaches that marriage is both unitive and procreative, and that it is inseparably both.

---

10   Pope John Paul II, *On the Dignity and Vocation of Women* (*Mulieris Dignitatem* [MD]) (Washington, DC: USCCB, 1998), no. 7.

11   MD, no. 7.

Unitive

Pope John Paul II's theology of the body speaks of the human body as having a spousal significance. This means that the human body by its very nature signifies that we humans are directed to relationship—that we are to seek union with others. For it is only in relationship that we achieve a true wholeness as a communion of persons. Before Eve was created, Adam was alone. His joy upon perceiving Eve indicated that with Eve he achieved the "original unity" that human nature seeks. God clearly made human beings to love and to be loved, to be in relationships wherein the act of giving oneself and receiving the other becomes complete.

In this context, the word "original" means not only that these experiences go back to the dawn of human history but, more importantly, that they are key to understanding our most basic human experiences. The experience of Adam and Eve speaks powerfully to our search not only to understand ourselves but also to love and be loved, to be in a relationship of love with a person of the opposite sex.

God established marriage so that man and woman could participate in his love and thus selflessly give themselves to each other in love. A man and a woman who by their act of consent are no longer two but one flesh (see Mt 19:6ff.) render mutual help and service to each other through an intimate union of their persons and of their actions.[12]

"My lover belongs to me and I to him" (Song 2:16; see Song 6:3). With all the dignity and simplicity of poetry, the Bride in the Song of Songs sings of the unitive meaning of married love.

"You have ravished my heart, my sister, my bride. . . . How beautiful is your love!" (Song 4:9-10). So responds the Bridegroom of the Song, overcome with the wonder of conjugal love that is extended to him by the Bride.[13] This is the love that is strong as death (see Song 8:6b).

---

12   See GS, no. 48.

13   See Pope John Paul II, General Audience, May 30, 1984.

Just as beautifully, Tobiah prays with his wife, Sarah, on their wedding night, awestruck at the mercy of the God of their fathers, that is, the God of the covenant, in bringing them together in a union of true conjugal love:

> Blessed are you, O God of our fathers;
>> praised be your name forever and ever.
> Let the heavens and all your creation praise you forever.
> You made Adam and you gave him his wife Eve
>> to be his help and support;
>> and from these two the human race descended.
> You said, "It is not good for the man to be alone;
>> let us make him a partner like himself."
> Now, Lord, you know that I take this wife of mine
>> not because of lust,
>> but for a noble purpose.
> Call down your mercy on me and on her,
>> and allow us to live together to a happy old age. (Tb 8:5-7)

The love that is as strong as death is the love that prays and praises, caught up into divine love.[14]

Procreative

It is the nature of love to overflow, to be life-giving. Thus, it is no surprise that marriage is ordained not only to growing in love but to transmitting life: "by its very nature the institution of marriage and married love [is] ordered to the procreation and education of the offspring and it is in them that it finds its crowning glory."[15]

Married love itself is ordered to the procreation of children, for, after all, the first command given to Adam and Eve is "be fertile and multiply" (Gn 1:28). Tobiah's prayer, even as it asks for a happy and lifelong union, remembers that the human race descended from Adam and Eve. His prayer for happiness certainly

---

14   See GS, no. 48: "Authentic married love is caught up into divine love."

15   GS, no. 48; see CCC, no. 1652.

includes, even if implicitly, a prayer for offspring. God indeed sends the couple seven sons (Tb 14:3) and long life (Tb 14:14). Again, in the words of the Second Vatican Council:

> Children are the supreme gift of marriage. . . . Without intending to underestimate the other ends of marriage, it must be said that true married love and the family life which flows from it have this end in view: that the spouses would cooperate generously with the love of the Creator and Savior, who through them will in due time increase and enrich his family.[16]

Children are a gift in a myriad of ways. They bring joy even in the midst of heartaches; they give added direction to the lives of their parents. Children, who are the fruit of love and meaningful commitment, are a cause of love and meaning.

It is true that some marriages will not result in procreation due to infertility, even though the couple is capable of the natural act by which procreation takes place. Indeed, this situation often comes as a surprise and can be a source of deep disappointment, anxiety, and even great suffering for a husband and wife. When such tragedy affects a marriage, a couple may be tempted to think that their union is not complete or truly blessed. This is not true. The marital union of a man and a woman is a distinctive communion of persons. An infertile couple continues to manifest this attribute.

Even when their child-bearing years have passed, a couple should continue to be life-affirming. They can do this by staying involved in the lives of young people, and especially their grandchildren, as spiritual mentors, teachers, and wisdom figures. They can also continue to be nurturing through the exercise of care for those who are needy, disabled, or pushed to the margins of society, and by their support for or participation in works of charity and justice.

---

16   GS, no. 50; see CCC, no. 1652.

How Are the Two Ends
of Marriage Related?

The Church speaks of an inseparable connection between the two ends of marriage: the good of the spouses themselves as well as the procreation of children. The *Catechism of the Catholic Church* teaches that "these two meanings or values of marriage cannot be separated without altering the couple's spiritual life and compromising the goods of marriage and the future of the family."[17] This inseparability arises from the very nature of conjugal love, a love that "stands under the twofold obligation of fidelity and fecundity."[18]

Conjugal love expresses the unitive meaning of marriage in such a way as to show how this meaning is ordered toward the equally obvious procreative meaning. The unitive meaning is distorted if the procreative meaning is deliberately disavowed. Conjugal love is then diminished. This love is, by its nature, faithful, exclusive, and intended to be fecund. As Pope Paul VI says, "It is not confined wholly to the loving interchange of husband and wife; it also contrives to go beyond this to bring new life into being."[19] Without its ordering toward the procreative, the unitive meaning of marriage is undermined.

Likewise, the procreative meaning of marriage is degraded without the unitive. If someone were to view his or her spouse simply as a way of producing offspring, with no loving attentiveness to the spouse's own good or fulfillment, this would offend against the human value of the procreative meaning.

The procreative meaning of marriage involves not only the conception of children, but also their upbringing and education, including spiritual formation in the life of love. This formation can take place only within a human community formed in love.

---

17   CCC, no. 2363.

18   CCC, no. 2363.

19   Pope Paul VI, *On the Regulation of Birth* (*Humanae Vitae* [HV]), no. 9, *www.vatican. va/holy_father/paul_vi/encyclicals/documents/hf_p-vi_enc_25071968_humanae-vitae_ en.html*.

The loving communion of the spouses is the primary context in which children are both conceived and brought up in love.

The unitive and the procreative purposes are meant to be inseparable. In this way, the procreative requires the unitive, just as the unitive is ordered to the procreative. These are two connected meanings of the same reality.

We can better understand this intrinsic connection if we consider the fact that procreation is a participation in the ongoing creative activity of God. The *Catechism of the Catholic Church* states that God's creative power is not a power of force or manipulation, but a power of love.[20] It is a power of self-gift. God is eternally happy in himself because he is a loving communion of three persons. He is self-sufficient and needs nothing else to be happy. Yet he wills to share his life and happiness with creatures who would have no existence were it not for this creative self-gift. Participating in the creative work of God means participating in the self-emptying or self-giving love of God, the rendering of one's whole being into a gift. If procreation is a true participation in the creative activity of God, it is a work that is inseparable from self-gift.

In the case of marriage, the principal and original self-gift is the unitive, mutual self-gift of the spouses to each other. In their marriage promises, the spouses pledge love and fidelity for as long as they live. The transmission of life is a sublime, concrete realization of this radical self-gift between a man and a woman. The mutual married love of man and woman "becomes an image of the absolute and unfailing love with which God loves man[kind],"[21] because as mutual self-gift, it is at the same time creative self-gift. The unitive and the procreative meanings of marriage are joined because they are two aspects of the same self-giving.

---

20   CCC, no. 2363.

21   CCC, no. 1604.

Fundamental Challenges to the Nature and Purposes of Marriage

We recognize that couples face many challenges to building and sustaining a strong marriage. Conditions in contemporary society do not always support marriage. For example, many couples struggle to balance home and work responsibilities; others bear serious economic and social burdens.

Some challenges, however, are fundamental in the sense that they are directed at the very meaning and purposes of marriage. Here we want to discuss four such challenges: contraception, same-sex unions, divorce, and cohabitation.

1. Contraception

Just as there are two inseparable purposes of marriage as a whole, the same is true of the act most symbolic and expressive of the marriage as a whole, namely, the act of sexual intercourse. Church teaching speaks of an "inseparable connection, established by God, which man on his own initiative may not break, between the unitive significance and the procreative significance which are both inherent to the marriage act."[22]

Sometimes one hears it said that as long as the marriage as a whole is open to children, each individual act of intercourse need not be. In fact, however, a marriage is only as open to procreation as each act of intercourse is, because the whole meaning of marriage is present and signified in each marital act. Each marital act signifies, embodies, and renews the original and enduring marital covenant between husband and wife. That is what makes intercourse exclusively a *marital* act. Engaging in marital intercourse is speaking the "language of the body," as Pope John Paul II calls it—a language of personal communion in complete and mutual self-donation.[23]

---

22   HV, no. 12; CCC, no. 2366.

23   See, for example, Pope John Paul II, General Audiences, January 5 and 26, 1983.

The spouses' mutual promise of lifelong love and fidelity provides this act with the clarity of an explicitly stated intention that enables the language of the body to be spoken. It is the intention of both spouses to cling together for life as "one flesh," in a completely mutual self-gift that gives the language of the body its voice. In each marital act, this intention is signified, or "spoken." Each marital act signifies the grateful openness to all of God's gifts. When the act signifies this grateful openness, one gives oneself completely, without shame (see Gn 2:25).

Deliberately intervening, by the use of contraceptive practices, to close off an act of intercourse to the possibility of procreation is a way of separating the unitive meaning of marriage from the procreative meaning. This is objectively wrong in and of itself and is essentially opposed to God's plan for marriage and proper human development. It makes the act of intercourse signify, or speak, something less than the unreserved self-gift intended in the marriage promises. The language of the body that is meant to express self-gift becomes mixed with another message, a contrary message—namely, the refusal to give oneself entirely. Thus the unitive meaning of that language is falsified.[24]

"By using contraception," married couples "may think that they are avoiding problems or easing tensions, that they are exerting control over their lives."[25] At the same time, they may think that they are doing nothing harmful to their marriages. In reality, the deliberate separation of the procreative and unitive meanings of marriage has the potential to damage or destroy the marriage. Also, it results in many other negative consequences, both personal and social.

Conjugal love is diminished whenever the union of a husband and wife is reduced to a means of self-gratification. The procreative capacity of male and female is dehumanized, reduced to a kind of internal biological technology that one masters and controls just like any other technology. Pope Paul VI warns

---

24 See FC, no. 32; see also CCC, no. 2370.

25 USCCB, *Married Love and the Gift of Life* (Washington, DC: USCCB, 2006), 17.

against treating the sexual faculties as simply one more technology to control:

> to experience the gift of married love while respecting the laws of conception is to acknowledge that one is not the master of the sources of life but rather the minister of the design established by the Creator. Just as man does not have unlimited dominion over his body in general, so also, and with more particular reason, he has no such dominion over his specifically sexual faculties, for these are concerned by their very nature with the generation of life, of which God is the source.[26]

The procreative capacity of man and woman should not be treated as just another means of technology, as also happens with *in vitro* fertilization (IVF) or cloning. When that happens, human life itself is degraded because it becomes, more and more, something produced or manufactured in various ways, ways that will only multiply as science advances. Children begin to be seen less as gifts received in a personal communion of mutual self-giving, and increasingly as a lifestyle choice, a commodity to which all consumers are entitled. There is a true issue of the dignity of human life at stake here. In this context, the warning of Pope Paul VI seems prophetic in retrospect:

> In preserving intact the whole moral law of marriage, the Church is convinced that she is contributing to the creation of a truly human civilization. She urges man not to betray his personal responsibilities by putting all his faith in technical expedients. In this way she defends the dignity of husband and wife. . . . [and with it] "man's essential dignity."[27]

---

26 HV, no. 13.

27 HV, nos. 18 and 23, quoting Pope John XXIII, *On Christianity and Social Progress* (*Mater et Magistra*), 1961.

Finally, living according to God's design for love and life does not mean that married couples cannot plan their families. The principle of responsible parenthood describes the way spouses can work with God's gift of fertility. Rooted in "the objective moral order which was established by God," spouses can "recognize their own duties towards God, themselves, their families and human society" as they decide when to try to achieve a pregnancy or conclude that there are sufficiently serious reasons to justify postponing one.[28] Today, the Church is particularly blessed that viable scientific methods of natural family planning are available to support responsible parenthood.

Natural family planning (NFP) methods represent authentic family planning. They can be used both to achieve and to postpone a pregnancy. NFP makes use of periodic abstinence from sexual intercourse based upon the observation of the woman's natural signs of fertility, in order to space births or to limit the number of children when there is a serious reason to do so. NFP methods require that couples learn, accept, and live with the wonders of how God made them. This is essentially different from contraception.

Openness to procreation in the marital act involves "acknowledg[ing] that one is not the master of the sources of life."[29] Using the technology of contraception is an attempt at such mastery. By contrast, couples using methods of NFP do nothing to alter the conjugal act. Rather, they abstain from conjugal relations during the portion of the woman's menstrual cycle when conception is most likely. This practice fosters in couples an attitude of respect and wonder in the face of human life, which is sacred. It also fosters profound respect for one's spouse, which is necessary for the mutual enjoyment of authentic intimacy.

As Pope John Paul II observes, any couple who tries to live out this openness to procreation will find that it requires a sacrificial love.[30] At certain difficult times in life, the procreative mean-

---

28   HV, no. 10.

29   HV, no. 13.

30   See FC, no. 3.

ing of marriage may seem to be at odds with the unitive meaning. Though this can in fact never be the case, preserving unity may in some cases require a considerable sacrifice by couples. They should take heart from St. Paul's assurance that God will not test us beyond what we can endure: "God is faithful and will not let you be tried beyond your strength; but with the trial he will also provide a way out, so that you may be able to bear it" (1 Cor 10:13).

2. Same-Sex Unions

One of the most troubling developments in contemporary culture is the proposition that persons of the same sex can "marry." This proposal attempts to redefine the nature of marriage and the family and, as a result, harms both the intrinsic dignity of every human person and the common good of society.

Marriage is a unique union, a relationship different from all others. It is the permanent bond between one man and one woman whose two-in-one-flesh communion of persons is an indispensable good at the heart of every family and every society. Same-sex unions are incapable of realizing this specific communion of persons. Therefore, attempting to redefine marriage to include such relationships empties the term of its meaning, for it excludes the essential complementarity between man and woman, treating sexual difference as if it were irrelevant to what marriage is.

Male-female complementarity is intrinsic to marriage. It is naturally ordered toward authentic union and the generation of new life. Children are meant to be the gift of the permanent and exclusive union of a husband and a wife. A child is meant to have a mother and a father. The true nature of marriage, lived in openness to life, is a witness to the precious gift of the child and to the unique roles of a mother and father. Same-sex unions are incapable of such a witness. Consequently, making them equivalent to marriage disregards the very nature of marriage.[31]

---

31   See USCCB, *Between Man and Woman: Questions and Answers About Marriage and Same-Sex Unions* (Washington, DC: USCCB, 2003).

Jesus teaches that marriage is between a man and a woman. "Have you not read that from the beginning the Creator 'made them male and female' . . . For this reason a man shall leave his father and mother and be joined to his wife, and the two shall become one flesh" (Mt 19:4-6).

By attempting to redefine marriage to include or be made analogous with homosexual partnerships, society is stating that the permanent union of husband and wife, the unique pattern of spousal and familial love, and the generation of new life are now only of relative importance rather than being fundamental to the existence and well-being of society as a whole.

Today, advocacy for the legal recognition of various same-sex relationships is often equated with non-discrimination, fairness, equality, and civil rights. However, it is not unjust to oppose legal recognition of same-sex unions, because marriage and same-sex unions are essentially different realities. "The denial of the social and legal status of marriage to forms of cohabitation that are not and cannot be marital is not opposed to justice; on the contrary, justice requires it."[32] To promote and protect marriage as the union of one man and one woman is itself a matter of justice. In fact, it would be a grave injustice if the state ignored the unique and proper place of husbands and wives, the place of mothers and fathers, and especially the rights of children, who deserve from society clear guidance as they grow to sexual maturity. Indeed, without this protection the state would, in effect, *intentionally* deprive children of the right to a mother and father.

The Church upholds the human dignity of homosexual persons, who are to "be accepted with respect, compassion, and sensitivity."[33] She also encourages all persons to have chaste friendships. "Chastity is expressed notably in *friendship with one's*

---

32 Congregation for the Doctrine of the Faith, *Considerations Regarding Proposals to Give Legal Recognition to Unions Between Homosexual Persons* (2003), no. 8, *www.vatican.va/roman_curia/congregations/cfaith/documents/rc_con_cfaith_doc_20030731_homosexual-unions_en.html.*

33 CCC, no. 2358.

neighbor. Whether it develops between persons of the same or opposite sex, friendship represents a great good for all."[34]

At the same time, the Church teaches that homosexual acts "are contrary to the natural law. They close the sexual act to the gift of life. They do not proceed from a genuine affective and sexual complementarity. Under no circumstances can they be approved."[35]

Basic human rights must be afforded to all people. This can and should be done without sacrificing the bedrock of society that is marriage and the family and without violating the religious liberty of persons and institutions.

The legal recognition of same-sex unions poses a multifaceted threat to the very fabric of society, striking at the source from which society and culture come and which they are meant to serve. Such recognition affects all people, married and non-married: not only at the fundamental levels of the good of the spouses, the good of children, the intrinsic dignity of every human person, and the common good, but also at the levels of education, cultural imagination and influence, and religious freedom.

3. Divorce

By its very nature, marriage is meant to be a lifelong covenantal union. Fidelity until death is what couples aspire to and what they promise to each other. Divorce, therefore, "claims to break the contract, to which the spouses freely consented, to live with each other till death."[36] Moreover, Jesus himself teaches that divorce does not accord with the binding nature of marriage as intended by the Creator (see Mt 19:3-9).

Conflict, quarrels, and misunderstandings can be found in all marriages. They reflect the impact of Original Sin, which

---

34 CCC, no. 2347.

35 CCC, no. 2357.

36 CCC, no. 2384.

"disrupted the original communion of man and woman."[37] They also reflect modern stresses upon marriage: the conflict between work and home, economic hardships, and social expectations.

Nevertheless, God's plan for marriage persists, and he continues to offer mercy and healing grace. We bishops urge couples in crisis to turn to the Lord for help. We also encourage them to make use of the many resources, including programs and ministries offered by the Church, that can help to save marriages, even those in serious difficulty.

In some cases, divorce may be the only solution to a morally unacceptable situation. A specific example is a home where the safety of a spouse and children is at risk. As the Catholic bishops of the United States, we reiterate what we said in our pastoral message on domestic violence, *When I Call for Help*, namely, that no one in a marriage is obliged to maintain common living with an abusing spouse.[38] We want to assure people who are caught in the tragedy of an abusive marriage that the Church is committed to offering them support and assistance.

We understand the pain of those for whom divorce seemed the only recourse. We urge them to make frequent use of the sacraments, especially the Sacraments of Holy Eucharist and Reconciliation. We also offer encouragement to those who have divorced and remarried civilly. Although the Church cannot recognize such subsequent unions as valid marriages, she hopes that people in this situation will participate in parish life and attend the Sunday Eucharist, even without receiving the Sacrament.

We encourage divorced persons who wish to marry in the Catholic Church to seek counsel about the options that exist to remedy their situation, including the suitability of a declaration of nullity when there is no longer any hope of reconciliation of the spouses. Such a declaration is a finding by a church tribunal,

---

37   USCCB, *United States Catholic Catechism for Adults* (Washington, DC: USCCB, 2006), 287.

38   See USCCB, *When I Call for Help: A Pastoral Response to Domestic Violence Against Women* (Washington, DC: USCCB, 2002), 11.

or court, that no valid marriage bond was formed because the requirements for valid consent were not met at the time of the wedding. If a declaration of nullity is granted, and there are no other restrictions, both parties are free to marry in the Catholic Church. Although the purpose of this canonical process is to determine whether or not a marriage bond truly existed, nonetheless, the process can often result in healing and closure to a painful part of one's past.

4. Living Together Without Marriage

Today many couples are living together in a sexual relationship without the benefit of marriage. Many cohabiting couples believe that their desire for each other justifies the sexual relationship. This belief reflects a misunderstanding of the natural purpose of human sexual intercourse, which can only be realized in the permanent commitment of marriage. Sexual intercourse is meant to express the total and unrestricted gift of self that takes place in married love. To have sexual intercourse outside the covenant of marriage is gravely immoral because it communicates physically the gift of oneself to another when, at the same time, one is not willing or able to make a total and permanent commitment.

Couples offer various reasons for cohabiting, ranging from economics to convenience. Frequently, they have accepted the widespread societal belief that premarital cohabitation is a prudent way to determine whether they are truly compatible. They believe they need a trial period before proceeding to the lifelong commitment of marriage.

Social science research, however, finds that cohabitation has no positive effects on a marriage.[39] In some cases, cohabitation can in fact harm a couple's chances for a stable marriage. More importantly, though, cohabitation "involves the serious sin of

---

39   See David Popenoe and Barbara Dafoe Whitehead, "Should We Live Together?" (2002), *marriage.rutgers.edu/publicat.htm*.

fornication. It does not conform to God's plan for marriage and is always wrong and objectively sinful."[40]

Clearly, there is no substitute for the binding lifelong commitment of marriage, and by definition, there is certainly no way to "try it out." Only the public and legal commitment of marriage expresses the complete gift of self that is the basis of marriage.[41] To refuse the full commitment of marriage expresses something distinctly less than the unconditional trust required of complete self-giving.[42] At the heart of cohabitation lies a reluctance or refusal to make a public, permanent commitment. Young people need to develop the virtue required for sustaining such a lofty commitment.

Cohabitation can also have a negative impact on children. Many cohabiting couples bring children into the relationship, or children result from the relationship. The unstable nature of cohabitation puts these children at risk. With regard to the good of the children, a stable marriage between the parents is "the most human and humanizing context for welcoming children, the context which most readily provides emotional security and guarantees greater unity and continuity in the process of social integration and education."[43] The findings of the social sciences confirm that the best environment for raising children is a stable home provided by the marriage of their parents.[44]

---

40   *United States Catholic Catechism for Adults*, 410.

41   See Pontifical Council for the Family, *Family, Marriage, and "De Facto" Unions* (Washington, DC: USCCB, 2001), no. 25.

42   See *Family, Marriage, and "De Facto" Unions*, no. 25.

43   *Family, Marriage, and "De Facto" Unions*, no. 26.

44   See Institute for American Values, "Why Marriage Matters: Twenty-Six Conclusions from the Social Sciences," *www.americanvalues.org/html/r-wmm.html*.

Just as families render an invaluable service to society, society has a reciprocal obligation to protect and support families. The Second Vatican Council affirms that the well-being of society is closely tied to healthy marriages and families.[45] The *Catechism of the Catholic Church* explains:

> The family is the *original cell of social life*. It is the natural society in which husband and wife are called to give themselves in love and in the gift of life. Authority, stability, and a life of relationships within the family constitute the foundations for freedom, security, and fraternity within society.[46]

---

45   See GS, no. 47.

46   CCC, no. 2207.

PART TWO:
MARRIAGE IN THE
ORDER OF THE
NEW CREATION
The Sacrament of Matrimony

———————————— ∞ ————————————

In Part One, we discussed why and how the natural institution of marriage is a gift and blessing. Now, in Part Two, we will consider what it means to say that this natural institution has been raised by Christ to the dignity of a sacrament for Christians. If marriage is crucial to society on a natural level, it is also crucial to the Church on the supernatural level.

Married Life Affected by Original Sin

While marriage has remained the good gift that God created it to be, and so has not been a blessing forfeited because of the Fall, Original Sin has had grave consequences for married life. Because men and women became wounded by sin, marriage has become distorted. In the words of the *Catechism of the Catholic Church*,

> As a break with God, the first sin had for its first consequence the rupture of the original communion between man and woman. Their relations were distorted by mutual recriminations; their mutual attraction, the Creator's own gift, changed into a relationship of domination and lust; and the beautiful

vocation of man and woman to be fruitful, multiply, and subdue the earth was burdened by the pain of childbirth and the toil of work.[47]

Marriage Restored in Christ

Through Baptism, men and women are transformed, by the power of the Holy Spirit, into a new creation in Christ.[48] This new life in the Holy Spirit heals men and women from sin and elevates them to share in God's very own divine life. It is within this new Christian context that Jesus has raised marriage between the baptized to the dignity of a sacrament.[49] He heals marriage and restores it to its original purity of permanent self-giving in one flesh (see Mt 19:6).

In restoring to marriage its original meaning and beauty, Jesus proclaims what the Creator meant marriage to be "in the beginning." He does so because marriage will be made into the visible embodiment of his love for the Church. In his espousal of the Church as his Bride, he fulfills and elevates marriage. He reveals his own love "to the end" (Jn 13:1) as the purest and deepest love, the perfection of all love. In doing this he reveals the deepest meaning of all marital love: self-giving love modeled on God's inner life and love.

In marriage a man and a woman are united with each other, and the two become one flesh, so that they each love the other as they love themselves and cherish each other's bodies as their own. This union is an image of the relationship between Christ and his Church:

---

47   CCC, no. 1607, alluding to Gn 1:28, 2:22, 3:12, and 3:16-19.

48   See CIC, c. 849; CCEO, c. 675 §1.

49   See CIC, c. 1055 §1; CCEO, c. 776 §2. A valid marriage between any two validly baptized Christians, whether Catholic or not, is a sacrament. This includes marriages between a Catholic and a non-Catholic Christian, whether Orthodox or Protestant, although certain canonical requirements must be fulfilled for these marriages to be valid. A marriage between a Christian and an unbaptized person is still valid as a natural marriage, but is not a sacrament. Here, too, for a Catholic to enter such a marriage validly, certain canonical requirements must be fulfilled.

He who loves his wife loves himself. For no one hates his own flesh but rather nourishes and cherishes it, even as Christ does the church, because we are members of his body.

> "For this reason a man shall leave [his] father and
> [his] mother
> and be joined to his wife,
> and the two shall become one flesh."

This is a great mystery, but I speak in reference to Christ and the church. (Eph 5:28-32)

The Church Fathers expressed this truth when they described the relationship between Adam and Eve as a "type," or mysterious foreshadowing, of the relationship between Christ and the Church. The kind of relationship of love that is foreshadowed in the relationship between Adam and Eve is fulfilled in the relationship between Christ and his Church.

The Sacrament of Matrimony renews the natural institution of marriage and elevates it so that it shares in a love larger than itself. Marriage, then, is nothing less than a participation in the covenant between Christ and the Church. In the words of the Second Vatican Council,

> Spouses, therefore, are fortified and, as it were, consecrated for the duties and dignity of their state by [this] special sacrament; fulfilling their conjugal and family role by virtue of this sacrament, spouses are penetrated with the spirit of Christ and their whole life is suffused by faith, hope and charity; thus they increasingly further their own perfection and their mutual sanctification, and together they render glory to God.[50]

Because the call of Adam and Eve to become one flesh is realized on a more profound level in the creation of the Church

---

50   GS, no. 48.

as Christ's Bride, one can only see the depth of the meaning of marriage in relation to Christ and his love for the Church as his Bride. Marriage is a call to give oneself to one's spouse as fully as Christ gave himself to the Church. The natural meaning of marriage as an exchange of self-giving is not replaced, but fulfilled and raised to a higher level.

Christian Marriage as a Sacrament

Marriage is one of the Church's "mysteries," or sacraments. The *Catechism of the Catholic Church* puts it this way: "Christian marriage . . . becomes an efficacious sign, the sacrament of the covenant of Christ and the Church."[51] An "efficacious sign" is one that does not merely symbolize or signify something, but actually makes present what it signifies. Marriage signifies and makes present to baptized spouses the love of Christ by which he formed the Church as his spouse: "just as of old God encountered his people in a covenant of love and fidelity, so our Savior, the spouse of the church, now encounters Christian spouses through the sacrament of marriage."[52]

By using the image of the relationship between bridegroom and bride to explain the relationship between Christ and the Church, the Scriptures are appealing to a natural human relationship that is already well known. All of us know something about the depth, the intimacy, and the beauty of the gift of self that occurs in the marriage of husband and wife. The Scriptures also show us, however, that Christ's love for the Church surpasses natural human love. Christ's love for the Church is a love of complete self-giving. This love is most completely expressed by his death on the Cross. Christian marriage aspires not only to natural human love, but to Christ's love for the Church:

> Husbands, love your wives, even as Christ loved the church and handed himself over for her to sanctify her, cleansing her

---

51   CCC, no. 1617.

52   GS, no. 48.

by the bath of water with the word, that he might present to himself the church in splendor, without spot or wrinkle or any such thing, that she might be holy and without blemish. (Eph 5:25-27)

Christian spouses are called to this imitation of Christ, an imitation that is possible only because, in the Sacrament of Matrimony, the couple receives a participation in his love. As a sacrament, marriage signifies and makes present in the couple Christ's total self-gift of love. Their mutual gift of self, conferred in their promises of fidelity and love *to the end*, becomes a participation in the *love to the end* by which Christ gave himself to the Church as to a Spouse (see Jn 13:1).

The baptized spouses are the ministers of the Sacrament of Matrimony. In addition, for marriages that are celebrated within the Latin Catholic Church, canonical form requires, among other things, that an authorized bishop, priest, or deacon ask for and receive the spouses' consent as the Church's official witness of the marriage celebration. For marriages of members of the Eastern Catholic Churches, the assistance and blessing of an authorized bishop or priest is required.[53] The Holy Spirit binds the spouses together through their exchange of promises in a bond of love and fidelity unto death. Their marriage covenant becomes a participation in the unbreakable covenant between Christ the Bridegroom and his Bride, the Church. The same love that defines the Church now defines the communion between the two spouses: "authentic married love is caught up into divine love and is directed and enriched by the redemptive power of Christ and the salvific action of the church."[54]

When Christian couples receive the grace of the Sacrament of Matrimony,

Christ dwells with them, gives them the strength to take up their crosses and so follow him, to rise again after they have

---

53   See CCC, no. 1623; CIC, cc. 1055, 1057, 1108; CCEO, cc. 776, 817, 828.

54   GS, no. 48.

fallen, to forgive one another, to bear one another's burdens, to "be subject to one another out of reverence for Christ," and to love one another with supernatural, tender, and fruitful love.[55]

By the power of the Holy Spirit, spouses become willing to do the acts and courtesies of love toward each other, regardless of the feelings of the moment. They are formed by the self-giving love of Christ for his Church as his Bride, and so they are enabled to perform acts of self-giving love to the benefit of themselves, their families, and the whole Church. The Sacrament of Matrimony, like the Sacrament of Holy Orders, is a sacrament "directed toward the salvation of others; if [these sacraments] contribute as well to personal salvation, it is through service to others that they do so."[56] Those who receive these sacraments are given a special consecration in Christ's name to carry out the duties of their particular state in life.

The imitation of the love of Christ for the Church also calls for a healing of the relationship between man and woman. This should not be a one-sided subjection of the wife to the husband, but rather a mutual subjection of husband and wife. St. Paul did indeed speak in a way that, according to Pope John Paul II, was "profoundly rooted in the customs and religious tradition of the time": "wives should be subordinate to their husbands as to the Lord" (Eph 5:22). The Holy Father explains, however, that this saying must "be understood and carried out in a new way," that is, in light of what St. Paul said immediately before: "be subordinate to one another out of reverence for Christ" (Eph 5:21). He emphasizes that this is something new, "an innovation of the Gospel," that has challenged and will continue to challenge the succeeding generations after St. Paul.[57]

---

55   CCC, no. 1642.

56   CCC, no. 1534.

57   See MD, no. 24.

Marriage as a Reflection of the Life of the Trinity

Throughout history God has shown us his selfless love. In espousing himself to the Church in sacrificial, life-giving love, Christ reveals the Father's love in the power of the Holy Spirit. He shows us the inner life of the Holy Trinity, a communion of persons, Father, Son, and Holy Spirit. The Church herself is a communion of persons that shares in God's Trinitarian life and love.

> The mystery of the Most Holy Trinity is the central mystery of Christian faith and life. It is the mystery of God in himself. It is therefore the source of all the other mysteries of faith, the light that enlightens them. It is the most fundamental and essential teaching in the "hierarchy of the truths of faith."[58]

Through the Sacrament of Matrimony, married love not only is modeled on Trinitarian love but also participates in it. Like all sacraments, Matrimony draws believers more deeply into the Trinitarian life of God. It was not until the Father sent his Son into the world as man, and the subsequent outpouring of the Holy Spirit, that the full identity of God as a Trinity of Persons was revealed. This Revelation not only allowed humankind to come to a definitive knowledge of God—since the mystery of the Trinity is the source of all the other mysteries, the revelation of this mystery sheds light on all the rest. This includes both the mystery that human beings are created in the image and likeness of God and the mystery that is marriage and family life.

As we learn from the mystery of the Trinity, to be in the image and likeness of God is not simply to have intelligence and free will, but also to live in a communion of love. From all eternity the Father begets his Son in the love of the Spirit. In the begetting of the Son, the Father gives himself entirely over to the Son in the love of the Holy Spirit. The Son, having been begotten of the

---

58   CCC, no. 234.

Father, perfectly returns that love by giving himself entirely over to the Father in the same Spirit of love. It is because he is begotten of the Father, and loves the Father in the same Spirit, that he is called Son. The Holy Spirit is then acknowledged as the mutual love of the Father for his Son and of the Son for his Father. This is why the Spirit is known as the gift of love.

Here one can see that the Father, the Son, and the Holy Spirit give themselves entirely to one another in a life-giving exchange of love. Thus, the Trinity is a loving and life-giving communion of equal Persons. The one God is the loving inter-relationship of the Father, the Son, and the Holy Spirit.

To be created in the image and likeness of God means, therefore, that human beings reflect not the life of a solitary deity, but the communal life of the Trinity. Human beings were created not to live solitary lives, but to live in communion with God and with one another, a communion that is both life-giving and loving. "The divine image is present in every man. It shines forth in the communion of persons, in the likeness of the unity of the divine persons among themselves."[59]

On a basic level this is witnessed in the social nature of human beings. We live in societies for the mutual benefit of all. "All men are called to the same end: God himself. There is a certain resemblance between the unity of the divine persons and the fraternity that men are to establish among themselves in truth and love. Love of neighbor is inseparable from love of God."[60] In the smaller community of the married couple and their family, the image of the Trinity can be seen even more clearly. Here are two ways to see the Trinitarian image in marriage and family life.

First, like the Persons of the Trinity, marriage is a communion of love between co-equal persons, beginning with that between husband and wife and then extending to all the members of the family. Pope John Paul II teaches, "The family, which is founded

---

59   CCC, no. 1702.

60   CCC, no. 1878.

and given life by love, is a community of persons: of husband and wife, of parents and children, of relatives."[61]

This communion of life-giving love is witnessed within the life of the family, where parents and children, brothers and sisters, grandparents and relatives are called to live in loving harmony with one another and to provide mutual support to one another. The *Catechism of the Catholic Church* teaches that "the Christian family is a communion of persons, a sign and image of the communion of the Father and the Son in the Holy Spirit."[62]

These relations among the persons in communion simultaneously distinguish them from one another and unite them to one another. For example, the Father is only the Father in relation to the Son and the Holy Spirit. Therefore, just as the Father, the Son, and the Holy Spirit are distinctly who they are only in relation to one another, so a man and a woman are distinctly who they are as husband and wife only in relation to one another. At the same time, in a way analogous to the relations among Father, Son, and Holy Spirit, which unites the three persons as one God, the inter-relationship of the husband and wife make them one as a married couple.

The Trinitarian image in marriage and family life can be seen in a second way. Just as the Trinity of persons is a life-giving communion of love both in relationship to one another and to the whole of creation, so a married couple shares in this life-giving communion of love by together procreating children in the conjugal act of love. For St. Thomas Aquinas, while angels are, strictly speaking, higher than human beings by nature, the ability to procreate in love makes human beings, at least in one way, more in the image and likeness of God than the angels, who are unable to procreate. In human beings one finds "a certain imitation of God, consisting in the fact that man proceeds from man, as God proceeds from God."[63]

---

61   FC, no. 18.

62   CCC, no. 2205.

63   Thomas Aquinas, *Summa Theologiae*, I, q. 93, art. 3, in *Fathers of the English Dominican Province* (New York: Benziger Brothers, 1947).

The Family as Domestic Church

The Christian family is a communion of persons, a sign and image of the communion of the Father and the Son in the Holy Spirit. In the procreation and education of children it reflects the Father's work of creation. It is called to partake of the prayer and sacrifice of Christ. Daily prayer and the reading of the Word of God strengthen it in charity. The Christian family has an evangelizing and missionary task.[64]

Although the Son of God was conceived in the womb of the Virgin Mary, becoming man by the power of the Holy Spirit, he was nonetheless born into a genuine human family. While Mary was his true mother, Joseph, as her husband, was the father of Jesus in the eyes of the law. It would be in living with Mary and Joseph that Jesus would learn to pray to his heavenly Father, to read and study the Scriptures, and in general to live as a devout Jewish man. With his family Jesus would attend the local synagogue and make the annual pilgrimage to Jerusalem for Passover. By being obedient to Mary and Joseph, "Jesus advanced [in] wisdom and age and favor before God and man" (Lk 2:52). It is within the context of his family that Jesus would come to know as man the will of his heavenly Father, who had sent him into the world to be its Savior and Redeemer. In contemplating the Jewish family of Joseph, Mary, and Jesus, people today can understand how this Holy Family is indeed the model and source of inspiration for all Christian families.

From the earliest days of the Church, entire families and households found salvation in Jesus. Cornelius, the first Gentile Christian, was told by an angel to send for Peter so that "all your household will be saved" (Acts 11:14). Paul and Silas preached the Gospel to their former jailer and his household. "Then he and

---

64   CCC, no. 2205.

all his family were baptized at once" (Acts 16:33). In Corinth, "Crispus, the synagogue official, came to believe in the Lord along with his entire household" (Acts 18:8). The *Catechism of the Catholic Church* states, "These families who became believers were islands of Christian life in an unbelieving world."[65] As the first Christian families were islands of faith in their time, so Catholic families today are called to be beacons of faith, "centers of living, radiant faith."[66]

Through the Sacrament of Matrimony, Christian couples are configured to Christ's love for the Church. Because of this participation in the love of Christ, the communion of persons formed by the married couple and their family is a kind of microcosm of the Church. For this reason, the Second Vatican Council employs the ancient expression "domestic church," *ecclesia domestica*, to describe the nature of the Christian family.[67] The family is called a "domestic church" because it is a small communion of persons that both draws its sustenance from the larger communion that is the whole Body of Christ, the Church, and also reflects the life of the Church so as to provide a kind of summary of it.

Pope John Paul II states, "The Christian family constitutes a specific revelation and realization of ecclesial communion, and for this reason . . . it can and should be called a *domestic church*."[68] As the Church is a community of faith, hope, and love, so the Christian family, as the domestic church, is called to be a community of faith, hope, and love. Through this faith, hope, and love, Jesus, by the power of his Holy Spirit, abides within each Christian family, as he does within the whole Church, and pours out the love of his Father within it. Every marriage between Christians gives rise to a domestic church, though marriages between two Catholics most

---

65   CCC, no. 1655.

66   CCC, no. 1656.

67   See Vatican Council II, *Dogmatic Constitution on the Church* (*Lumen Gentium* [LG]), no. 11.

68   FC, no. 21.

fully reflect the life of the Church, because ordinarily only Catholic couples can fully participate in the sacraments of the Church, including the Eucharist.[69]

While all members of the family are called to live out the foundational Christian virtues, fathers and mothers have a special responsibility for fostering these virtues within their children. They are the first to proclaim the faith to their children. They are responsible for nurturing the vocation of each child, showing by example how to live the married life, and taking special care if a child might be called to priesthood or consecrated life.[70]

Not only do parents present their children for Baptism, but, having done so, they become the first evangelizers and teachers of the faith.[71] They evangelize by teaching their children to pray and by praying with them. They bring their children to Mass and teach them biblical stories. They show them how to obey God's commandments and to live a Christian life of holiness. Catholic schools, religious education programs, and Catholic homeschooling resources can help parents fulfill these responsibilities.

Cooperating together, with the help of the Holy Spirit, parents nurture the virtues within each of their children and within their family as a whole—charity, joy, peace, patience, kindness, generosity, faithfulness, gentleness, and self-control (see Gal 5:22-23). The *Catechism of the Catholic Church*, quoting the Second Vatican Council, emphasizes that the family, as a domestic church, receives its strength and life by participating in the life and worship of the larger Church of which it is a part:

> It is here [within the domestic church] that the father of the family, the mother, children, and all members of the family exercise the *priesthood of the baptized* in a privileged way "by the reception of the sacraments, prayer and thanksgiving,

---

69 See CIC, c. 844; Pontifical Council for Promoting Christian Unity, *Directory for the Application of Principles and Norms on Ecumenism* (Washington, DC: USCCB, 1993), nos. 125, 131.

70 See LG, no. 11.

71 See CIC, cc. 226 §2, 774 §2, 793, 867 §1, 1125 1°; CCEO, cc. 618, 627, 686 §1, 814 1°.

the witness of a holy life, and self-denial and active charity" (LG, no. 10). Thus the home is the first school of Christian life and "a school for human enrichment" (GS, no. 52). Here one learns endurance and the joy of work, fraternal love, generous—even repeated—forgiveness, and above all divine worship in prayer and the offering of one's life.[72]

A family matures as a domestic church as it ever more deeply immerses itself within the life of the Church. This especially means that fathers and mothers, by their example and teaching, help their children come to an appreciation of the need for continual conversion and repentance from sin, encouraging a love for and participation in the Sacrament of Reconciliation.

Moreover, since it is Christ's presence within the family that truly makes it a domestic church, their participation in the Eucharist, especially the Sunday Eucharist, is particularly important. In the Eucharist, the family joins itself to Jesus' sacrifice to the Father for the forgiveness of sins. Furthermore, it is in receiving Holy Communion that the members of the family are most fully united to the living and glorious Christ and so to one another and to their brothers and sisters throughout the world. It is here, in the risen and Eucharistic Christ, that spouses, parents, and children express and nurture most fully the love of the Father and the bond of the Spirit.

Although Christian spouses in a mixed marriage (that is, between a Catholic and a baptized person who is not Catholic) do not ordinarily share the Eucharist,[73] they are called to "give witness to the universality of God's love which overcomes all division."[74]

These families may experience the wounds of Christian division, yet they can also contribute to healing those wounds. When

---

72   CCC, no. 1657.

73   See CIC, c. 844; *Directory for the Application of Principles and Norms on Ecumenism*, nos. 125, 131.

74   USCCB, *Follow the Way of Love: A Pastoral Message to Families* (Washington, DC: USCCB, 1993), 11.

the two spouses live together in peace, they provide a reminder to all Christians that progress toward the unity for which Christ prayed is possible. Mixed marriages can, therefore, make an important contribution towards Christian unity. This is especially true "when spouses are faithful to their religious duties. Their common baptism and the dynamism of grace provide the spouses in these marriages with the basis and motivation for expressing their unity in the sphere of moral and spiritual values."[75]

Catholics sometimes enter into valid marriages with persons of other religions that do not profess faith in Christ. Because such marriages may make more difficult a Catholic's perseverance in the faith, the Catholic party is required, after much discernment with his or her intended spouse as to the wisdom of their marrying, to obtain a dispensation to be married in the Church. Such a marriage to a non-baptized person is not a sacrament—although parties do commit to fidelity, permanence, and openness to children.

It is important to recognize the religious and cultural pressures that sometimes make it difficult for the Catholic party to share his or her faith with the children. The Catholic party needs to take seriously the obligations imposed by faith, especially in regard to the religious upbringing of children. The Church requires the Catholic party to be faithful to his or her faith and to "promise to do all in his or her power"[76] to have the children baptized and raised in the Catholic faith. The non-Catholic spouse is "to be informed at an appropriate time about the promises which the Catholic party is to make, in such a way that it is certain that he or she is truly aware of the promise and obligation of the Catholic party."[77]

In the United States, religiously mixed marriages have become increasingly common. While recognizing that other faith communities hold marriage as a sacred institution that contributes to the building of civilization, the Catholic Church also cautions that these unions face particular challenges that must be met with realism and reliance on the grace of God.

---

75   FC, no. 78.

76   CIC, c. 1125, 2°.

77   CIC, c. 1125.

Marriage as a Vocation

God who created man out of love also calls him to love—the fundamental and innate vocation of every human being.[78]

The Church teaches that marriage is an authentic vocation, or divine call. As a vocation, marriage is just as necessary and valuable to the Church as other vocations. For this reason, all of us should pray that men and women will enter into marriage with the proper understanding and motivation and that they will live it generously and joyfully.

As with every vocation, marriage must be understood within the primary vocation to love, because humanity "is created in the image and likeness of God who is himself love."[79] In Baptism, God calls the faithful to grow in love. This vocation to love, in imitation of God's infinite love, is also a vocation to grow in holiness, for greater participation in God's love necessarily entails a greater participation in God's holiness. The Second Vatican Council teaches that "all the faithful, whatever their condition or state are called by the Lord—each in his or her own way—to that perfect holiness by which the Father himself is perfect."[80] Within this universal vocation to holiness, God calls some men to the priesthood or to the diaconate, other men and women to the consecrated life. For the vast majority of men and women, however, God places this universal vocation to holiness within the specific vocation of marriage. Those whose circumstances in life do not include marriage, ordination, or consecration are nonetheless also called to discern and make a personal gift of self in how they live a Christian life.

How do men and women discern a call to marriage? Discernment of and preparation for marriage begins early in life. *Familiaris Consortio* identifies three stages of marriage preparation:

---

78   CCC, no. 1604.

79   CCC, no. 1604.

80   LG, no. 11; see CIC, c. 210; CCEO, c. 13.

remote, proximate, and immediate.[81] *Remote* preparation occurs early in life, as children experience the love and care of married parents and begin to learn the values and virtues that will form their character. *Proximate* preparation begins around puberty and involves a more specific preparation for the sacraments, including an understanding of healthy relationships, sexuality, the virtue of chastity, and responsible parenthood.

By the time of *immediate* preparation, the couple has developed a conviction that God is calling them to marriage with a particular person. Prayer, especially for the guidance of the Holy Spirit, and the help of wise mentors are crucial in this discernment process. Discernment also involves an honest assessment of qualities that are foundational for the marriage. These include an ability to make and keep a commitment, the desire for a lifelong, faithful relationship, and openness to children. The couple will also want to reflect on the values they share, their ability to communicate, and agreement on significant issues.

The marital vocation is not a private or merely personal affair. Yes, marriage is a deeply personal union and relationship, but it is also for the good of the Church and the entire community. The Second Vatican Council teaches that "the well-being of the individual person and of both human and Christian society is closely bound up with the healthy state of marriage and the family."[82] As a vocation, or call from God, marriage has a public and ecclesial status within the Church. Catholic spouses ordinarily exchange marital consent within a church setting, before a priest or deacon.[83] The living-out of marriage takes place within the whole Body of Christ, which it serves and in which it finds nourishment.

Moreover, the state and the secular community officially recognize a couple's marital and familial status and are obliged to help support and sustain it. The ecclesial and public nature of marriage and family life is what keeps marriages and families from

---

81   See FC, no. 66.

82   GS, no. 47.

83   See CIC, c. 1108; CCEO, c. 828.

becoming isolated. Marriage and families are compelled, by their very nature, to contribute to the life of the Church and to the broader needs of society.

Growth in Christian Marriage

On their wedding day, the couple says a definitive "yes" to their vocation of marriage. Then the real work of marriage begins. For the remainder of their married lives, the couple is challenged to grow, through grace, into what they already are: that is, an image of Christ's love for his Church.[84]

"Become what you are!"[85] might be a great exhortation to newly married couples, especially given the strong tendency nowadays to reduce the love of the marriage bond to only a feeling, perhaps the romantic love of courtship and honeymoon. When that feeling dries up, it may seem to them that they have nothing left and that they have failed.

It is at these very times, however, that their vocation as spouses calls them to go further, to "become what they are," members of a marital communion defined by the unbreakable spousal love of Christ for his Church. While husbands and wives can cling to the unconditional promise that they made at their wedding as a source of grace, this will require persistent effort. Maintaining the common courtesies—persevering in fidelity, kindness, communication, and mutual assistance—can become a deep expression of conjugal charity. It means growing in a love that is far deeper than a romantic feeling.

That growth will be the occasion of admiration and gratitude for the good Christian example of the other spouse and for the always undeserved gift of love. In this admiration and gratitude for the enduring and faithful love of one's spouse, one can see Christ, who loved to the end. One can also recognize Christ at work in oneself as a spouse.

---

84   See FC, no. 17.

85   FC, no. 17.

What about the physical expression of married love? Married couples tell us that at certain times in life marital intercourse does not seem as satisfying as it once seemed to be, and couples in this situation can come to think of themselves as having failed in the one thing that our secular culture tells us is essential. It may seem foolish or dreary to persist in a marriage that has come to seem unfulfilling. It is the consumerist-oriented version of sex, however, that is empty and inevitably unfulfilling, and that ultimately deadens sexual life.

Human beings attain their deepest fulfillment only by participation in the divine life of the Trinity, which comes through participation in the self-giving love pouring out of the pierced heart of Christ on the Cross. This fulfillment is exactly what the Sacrament of Matrimony offers.

The clarity of a promise of love to the end makes it possible for the spouses, in Christ, to achieve an intimacy where there is trust instead of shame. Leaving behind the lustful, self-centered pleasures of our culture, one can journey, in Christ, towards the discovery of an intimacy that is deeply satisfying because it is a participation in the intimate self-giving of Christ.

Growth in the Virtues

There is another way to look at growth in marriage: namely, as growth in virtue. As a couple grows in virtue, they grow in holiness. In other words, the couple acquires, by prayer and discipline, those interior qualities that open them to God's love and allow them to share in his love more deeply. Couples instinctively understand this when they speak about their marriage being a means of leading each other to heaven.

The vocation of marriage, like other vocations, is the living out of the theological virtues of faith, hope, and charity—those foundational virtues that each person receives from the Holy Spirit at Baptism and through which we all become holy. This means that a husband and wife are called to live their marriage in faith—faith in Jesus as their Lord and Savior and in accordance with the Church's teaching. They are to foster this gospel faith among themselves and within their children through their teaching and example.[86]

Likewise, they live in hope of God's kindness, mercy, and generosity. In the midst of the inevitable trials and hardships, they trust that God is graciously watching over them and their family. They trust that the Father's love will never abandon them, but that, in union with Jesus, they will always remain in his presence.

Faith and hope find their fullest expression in love—love of God and love of neighbor. The call to love reaches beyond the home to the extended family, the neighborhood, and the larger community. This marital and familial love finds its complete expression, following the example of Jesus himself, in a willingness to sacrifice oneself in everyday situations for one's spouse and children. There is no greater love within a marriage and a family than for the spouses and children to lay down their lives for one another. This is the heart of the vocation of marriage, the heart of the call to become holy.

Love in the Sacrament of Matrimony includes all the virtues, and each specific virtue is a manifestation of love. A holy marriage, one that is a communion of persons and a sign of God's love, is made up of many virtues that are acquired by human effort.

Rooted in the theological virtues, a couple must also grow in the principal moral virtues. These include prudence, justice, fortitude, and temperance. All the other virtues are grouped around these four. Practicing the moral virtues draws us ever more deeply into God's love through the Holy Spirit, with the result that we habitually manifest his love in our daily lives.

Chastity and *gratitude* are two virtues that are sometimes overlooked in relation to married life. These should be practiced in both natural and sacramental marriages.

---

86   See CIC, c. 226 §1; CCEO, c. 407.

Chastity

Everyone is called to chastity, whether married or not. The virtue of chastity is traditionally considered an expression of the virtue of temperance, which enables one to enjoy various kinds of pleasures when it is good and appropriate to do so, and to reject certain pleasures when it is not. Chastity is specifically concerned with the proper disposition of sexual desire. It refers to the peaceful integration of sexual thoughts, feelings, and desires.

Learning to live chastely is part of learning how to use one's freedom well. The *Catechism of the Catholic Church* teaches, "Chastity includes an *apprenticeship in self-mastery* which is a training in human freedom. The alternative is clear: either man governs his passions and finds peace, or he lets himself become dominated by them and becomes unhappy."[87]

Chastity will be lived somewhat differently depending on the circumstances of one's life. Single people, consecrated religious, and priests experience chastity differently from married persons. In fact, some people are surprised that married persons are called to chastity. They confuse chastity with celibacy or sexual abstinence, but marital chastity has a distinct meaning.

Married people are called to love with conjugal chastity. That is, their love is to be total, faithful, exclusive, and open to life.[88] Conjugal love merges "the human and the divine," leading the "partners to a free and mutual self-giving."[89] The practice of marital chastity ensures that both husband and wife will strive to live as a gift of self, one to the other, generously. In other words, marital chastity protects a great good: the communion of persons and the procreative purposes of marriage.

In this pastoral letter, we have already discussed how contraception threatens marital chastity. Other threats to marital chastity abound. In the workplace, men and women deal with boundary issues as they form professional relationships and per-

---

87   CCC, no. 2339.

88   See HV, no. 9.

89   GS, no. 49.

sonal friendships. Military deployments can strain marriages as they separate spouses for long periods of time.

Pornography, particularly Internet pornography, is a serious threat to marital chastity and is gravely immoral. The Internet has made pornography readily accessible within the privacy of one's home. Using pornography can quickly become an addiction that erodes trust and intimacy between husband and wife and, in some cases, leads to the breakup of the common life of the spouses.

A truly serious violation of marital chastity is adultery. It violates the marriage covenant and erodes the basic trust needed for a persevering total gift of self, one to the other. It is important that this be acknowledged as seriously sinful behavior, undermining the promised exclusive fidelity, sowing the seeds of marital breakdowns, and causing incredible harm to children.

A strong defense against these temptations is a marriage that is continually growing in physical, emotional, and spiritual intimacy. Communication and relationship skills are crucial to building such intimacy. As spouses learn to improve their communication, they can better respond to each other's need for love, acceptance, and appreciation. They deepen marital intimacy and strengthen their practice of chastity.

Gratitude

Adam's exclamation upon seeing Eve—"this one at last is bone of my bones and flesh of my flesh!" (Gn 2:23)—is one of joy. He expresses joy in receiving from God someone who is truly as human as he is, but who is different in a matching or complementary way. His joy is an expression of gratitude at receiving the gift of Eve. Eve, too, must have rejoiced upon seeing Adam, for she also saw someone who complemented her and was truly human like herself. This virtue of joyous gratitude is critical for marital and family love. Each married couple is called to foster this joyous gratitude—thankfulness that each is a gift to the other and that this gift of the other ultimately comes from God's bounteous love for them.

Within marriage the joyous gratitude is expressed, as it was for Adam and Eve, in the giving of one's whole self to the other. In joyful gratitude for his wife, a husband gives himself completely to his wife; and in gratitude for her husband, a wife gives herself completely to her husband. This joyful self-giving is specifically expressed and exemplified in sexual intercourse. As the Second Vatican Council teaches, "The acts in marriage by which the intimate and chaste union of the spouses takes place are noble and honorable; the truly human performance of these acts fosters the self-giving they signify and enriches the spouses in joy and gratitude."[90]

There is a second element to this gratitude that is related to the first. As a husband and wife are thankful for one another and express this gratitude in the giving of themselves completely to one another, so this gratitude is open to the further gifts that this self-giving literally embodies: that is, a gratitude for the possible further gift of children. Inherent within a husband's gratitude for his wife is that together with her he can beget children. Inherent within a wife's gratitude for her husband is that together with him she can conceive children. Together a husband and wife are gratefully open to the gift of children.

Marriage, then, is to be a school for nurturing gratitude for the gifts of God and for openness to the gifts of God that are proper to marriage. In practicing the virtue of gratitude and openness, spouses cooperate fully in the procreative task of married life: conceiving and educating children. Because the children are received in gratitude and in a spirit of openness to each of them as God's gifts, they are themselves formed in that very openness and in appreciation for all of those gifts. These gifts include life itself, the dignity of human beings created in the image and likeness of God, and the wondrous gift of the whole of the earth where all of life is nurtured and supported.

Moreover, the virtue of gratitude overflows from the marriage and family to embrace the Church and the world. With gratitude for their vocation to serve, married couples and their children are motivated to participate actively, in keeping with their indi-

---

90   GS, no. 49.

vidual talents and charisms, in the building-up of Christ's Body, the Church.

Lastly, living a married life in joyful gratitude and openness fosters hospitality. When the spouses become one flesh, their openness makes them a home to each other. Their communion with each other becomes a home for children, including adopted and foster children. Their family, with its heightened awareness of human dignity, reaches out in hospitality to the poor and to anyone in need, in keeping with the words of the final blessing from the ritual of weddings:

> May you always bear witness to the love of God in this world
> so that the afflicted and needy
> will find in you generous friends,
> and welcome you into the joys of heaven.[91]

Growth Toward Perfection

Some might object that growing in virtue—to be perfect as the Heavenly Father is perfect—is an unrealistic vision for married couples. After they are married, couples are still themselves, with all their personal faults and failings. Sacraments, each in their own way, really do configure us to the love of Christ revealed in his Passion, Death, and Resurrection (the Paschal Mystery), but they do not bring instant perfection.

In Baptism all of us are fully liberated from sin. We receive a new identity: "having become a member of the Church, the person baptized belongs no longer to himself, but to him who died and rose for us."[92] Yet our spiritual journey has only just begun in Baptism. We have to grow according to the love to which we have been configured. In Baptism we have been configured into the likeness of Christ so that we can grow in holiness of life and become increasingly conformed to his divine and resurrected likeness. We have to "become what we are."[93]

---

91 *Rite of Marriage* A, no. 125.

92 CCC, no. 1269; see 1 Cor 6:19, 2 Cor 5:15.

93 FC, no. 17.

While the Church is holy because of her union with the all-holy Christ, the spotless Bride of the spotless Lamb (see Rev 22:17), she is "always in need of purification."[94] Christ loves the Church "to the end" (Jn 13:1), and he continually purifies and reforms the Church. The Church is always called to "become what she already is," the holy Bride of Christ.

In a similar way, the Sacrament of Marriage configures the spouses into a sign of Christ's loving and unbreakable communion with his Bride, the Church. In their exchange of a promise of fidelity *to the end*, their communion becomes a participation in Jesus' everlasting spousal love for his Church.[95] By symbolizing and sharing in Christ's purifying and sanctifying love for his Church, married couples are called to an ever deeper holiness of life, just as Christ calls his Church to an ever deeper holiness of life.

Getting married does not, therefore, magically confer perfection. Rather, the love to which the spouses have been configured is powerful enough to transform their whole life's journey so that it becomes a journey toward perfection. In this journey, the spouses are ever more conformed into the likeness of Christ so that they can ever more perfectly love one another as Christ loves his Church.

Marriage and the Eucharist

[The Eucharist is] the memorial of the love with which he [Christ] loved us "to the end," even to the giving of his life. In his Eucharistic presence he remains mysteriously in our midst as the one who loved us and gave himself up for us.[96]

In the Eucharist, Catholic married couples meet the one who is the source of their marriage. "In this sacrifice of the new and eternal covenant, Christian spouses encounter the source from

---

94 CCC, no. 827.

95 See FC, no. 20.

96 CCC, no. 1380.

which their own marriage covenant flows, is interiorly structured and continuously renewed."[97] Pope Benedict XVI explains how, in the Eucharist, the very meaning of marriage is transfigured: "the imagery of marriage between God and Israel is now realized in a way previously inconceivable: it had meant standing in God's presence, but now it becomes union with God through sharing in Jesus' self-gift, sharing in his body and blood."[98]

Moreover, Pope Benedict points out that the sacramental mysticism he mentions is "social in character."[99] The Eucharist "makes the Church" because "those who receive the Eucharist are united more closely to Christ. Through it Christ unites them to all the faithful in one body—the Church."[100] In the Eucharist, spouses encounter the love that animates and sustains their marriage, the love of Christ for his Church. This encounter enables them to perceive that their marriage and family are not isolated units, but rather that they are to reach out in love to the broader Church and world of which they are a living part.

Marriage continually sends the believing Catholic back again to the Eucharist. Here is where the gratitude that has become a life-giving habit in a marriage can be fully and completely expressed. "Eucharist," after all, means "thanksgiving." In the Eucharist one thanks God the Father for his supreme gift, the gift of his risen Son, who, in turn, bestows most fully the divine life and love of the Holy Spirit.

Marriage is a school for gratitude. By celebrating the Sacrament of Marriage, "Christian spouses profess their gratitude to God for the sublime gift bestowed on them of being able to live in their married and family lives the very love of God for people and that of the Lord Jesus for the Church."[101]

---

97 FC, no. 57.

98 Pope Benedict XVI, *God Is Love* (*Deus Caritas Est* [DCE]) (Washington, DC: USCCB, 2006), no. 13.

99 DCE, no. 14.

100 CCC, no. 1396.

101 FC, no. 56.

Procreation and education, the basic and irreplaceable service of the family to society, are part of a formation in love and a formation for love that is a participation in building up the Kingdom of God.[102] Just as the Church is a "sacrament . . . of communion with God and of the unity of the entire human race,"[103] Christian marriage and the family contribute to the unity of humanity and to humanity's communion with God.

For example, since the Eucharist "commits us to the poor,"[104] so the hospitality of Christian marriage becomes enlarged as a commitment to the "preferential option for the poor"[105] by training each family member to recognize the image of God in each other, even the least. Thus, the natural virtue of marital hospitality is nourished and formed even more widely by the spouses' Eucharistic life.

Their hospitality, in turn, will build up the Church, making the Church a more hospitable or homelike place[106] and thereby an even stronger witness to Christ's love in the world. Thus, "the Christian family [that] springs from marriage . . . is an image and a sharing in the partnership of love between Christ and the Church; it will show to all people Christ's living presence in the world and the authentic nature of the church."[107]

Marriage Fulfilled in the Kingdom of God

A marriage that is truly in Christ, a marriage upon which his school of gratitude and openness has left its mark of joy and warmth, is a sign of the Kingdom that is coming. It is a blessing to the couple, to their children, and to everyone who knows them. It offers a sign of hope and a loving witness to human dignity in a world where hope often seems absent and human dignity is often

---

102 FC, no. 50.

103 LG, no. 1.

104 CCC, no. 1397.

105 FC, nos. 47, 64.

106 FC, no. 64.

107 GS, no. 48.

degraded. It is a sign of the Kingdom because the love of Christ moves the married couple to ever greater heights of love.

Christian married love is a preparation for eternal life. At the end of time, the love to which spouses have been called will find its completion when the entire Church is assumed into the glory of the risen Christ. Then the Church will truly be herself, for she will experience fully the self-giving love of her spouse—the Lord Jesus Christ.

This is the glorious wedding supper of the Lamb, to which the Spirit and the Bride say "Come!" (Rev 19:9, 22:17). Just as Christ once proclaimed the greatness of marriage by his presence at the wedding feast in Cana, so now, at the heavenly wedding banquet, marriage and all the blessings of the Holy Spirit, given to us by the Father through Christ, his Son, will find their ultimate consummation because we will be in perfect union with God.

A Commitment
to Ministry

In November 2004, we, as the United States Conference of Catholic Bishops, made a commitment to promote, strengthen, and protect marriage. We began a National Pastoral Initiative for Marriage in order to communicate from the riches of our Catholic faith the meaning and value of marriage and to offer support and practical assistance for it to flourish both in society and in the Church.

This pastoral letter extends and enriches the work of the National Pastoral Initiative for Marriage. It is a sign of our continuing commitment and of the priority we have given to marriage in the evangelizing mission of our bishops' conference. It is an expression of our esteem for the gift of married life and love that couples share so generously for the benefit of Church and society.

The Church is built on a foundation of marriage and family life, which it cherishes as the school of a deeper humanity and a cradle of the civilization of love. For this reason, both Pope John Paul II and Pope Benedict XVI have emphasized that pastoral ministry in service of marriage and family life should be an urgent priority for the Church.

We wish to echo and reinforce that message.

The vision of married life and love that we have presented in this pastoral letter is meant to be a foundation and reference point for the many works of evangelization, catechesis, pastoral care, education, and advocacy carried on in our dioceses, parishes, schools, agencies, movements, and programs.

WE URGE a renewed commitment by the entire Catholic community to helping those called to the vocation of married life to live it faithfully, fruitfully, and joyfully.

WE PLEDGE to be a marriage-building Church, drawing strength from God's grace while using creatively the gifts and resources entrusted to us.

WE CALL for a comprehensive and collaborative ministry to marriages. Because of the complexity and challenges we face in society today, our ministry must be one that

- **Proclaims and witnesses** to the fullness of God's Revelation about the meaning and mystery of marriage
- **Accompanies and assists** people at all stages of their journey: from the early years when young people begin to learn about committed relationships to the later years of married life, and even beyond them to grieving the loss of a spouse
- **Invites and includes** the gifts of many, beginning with married couples themselves and welcoming also the service and witness offered by ordained ministers and by women and men in consecrated life
- **Encourages and utilizes** many methods and approaches in order to serve individuals and couples whose circumstances in life, whose needs, and whose preparation and readiness to receive the Church's ministry can vary widely
- **Celebrates and incorporates** the diversity of races, cultures, ethnicity, and heritage with which God enriches the world and the Church especially in our nation

Finally, **WE ACKNOWLEDGE** with respect and gratitude all those who are working to defend, promote, strengthen, heal, and reconcile marriages, either through church ministries or in other professions and fields of endeavor. **WE PLEDGE** our collaboration with all who seek to create a vibrant culture of marriage rooted in God's plan for the good of humanity.

U.S. Catholic Bishops   November 2009